venus in fur

venus in fur

cocktails to bring out the animal in you

oliver hamilton

Published in 2010 by Max Press,
an imprint of Little Books Ltd,
Notting Hill, London W11 3QW

10 9 8 7 6 5 4 3 2 1

Text copyright © 20010 by Oliver Hamilton

Design and layout copyright © by Max Press

A CIP catalogue record for this book is available from the British Library.

ISBN 978 1 906251 40 6

Every attempt has been made to trace any copyright holders.
The author and publisher will be grateful for any information
that will assist them in keeping future editions up to date.
Although all reasonable care has been taken in the
preparation of this book, neither the publisher, editors
nor the author can accept any liability for any consequences
arising from the use thereof, or the information contained therein.

Printed and bound by Toppan Leefung, China

contents

introduction

the art of mixing

Drinking cocktails is about style, elegance and sophistication, but it is also about fun. Inspired by nature, nectar to the palate, the recipes chosen are also simple to make and require the minimum equipment. Many of those included have endured over the decades. Some are derived and adapted from Harry Craddock's classic *Savoy Cocktail Book*, published in 1930, and David Embury's *Fine Art of Mixing Drinks*, which appeared two decades later. Others are modern. All are guaranteed to make an entrance at any social occasion.

Although various technical terms are used in the preparation of a cocktail, there are essentially four ways of mixing a drink: shaken, blended, stirred or layered. Of all these methods, shaking is by the far the most common, intended to chill and dilute the ingredients as well as mixing them thoroughly together. A good shaker is a solid investment. If possible, use a standard threepiece shaker with a capacity of at least a pint and preferably made of stainless steel. For best results, firstly combine the ingredients in the base of the shaker, then fill it with roughly two thirds of ice. (This rule applies equally to blending, when a better result will be achieved if the liquid ingredients of the drink are placed in the blender first before the ice is added.) When shaking the cocktail always secure the top and cap. Then pick it up with one hand on top and the other gripping the bottom and shake vigorously for about twenty-five seconds.

When shaking, always direct away from your guests. Afterwards, remove the cap and pour through the strainer into the glass which ideally will have been already chilled in the fridge or freezer.

Occasionally, one of the recipes requires muddling, a term used by bartenders which refers to pummeling fresh fruit or herbs. A muddler is similar to a pestle, but any blunt instrument will do the job just as well. When muddling take care not to press too hard and if possible use a twisting action to ensure the maximum release of flavour and aroma. Layering different ingredients in a glass can take practice and patience. Every liquid varies in its density and weight. Syrups containing high sugar levels are most commonly the heaviest and line the bottom of a drink, but creamy liqueurs can be the lightest and usually 'float' well on top. For the best and most professional effect, slowly pour each layer of liquid over a bar or soup spoon onto the inside side of the glass.

staying cool

When preparing any cocktail, always ensure you have a plentiful supply of ice to hand. If you are making your own ice cubes it's best to avoid tap water if possible and use mineral water and filtered water to avoid any chemical or chlorine aftertaste. Be generous. If a recipe calls for an ice-filled glass, always fill it up to the top and don't just add a few cubes. Temperature is crucial to a truly refreshing drink. Luke-warm cocktails belong down the plug hole. When possible use a pre-chilled frosty glass straight from the freezer. If you are in a rush, fill the glass with ice and water and put it to one side while you are mixing the ingredients. If available, use ice made from filtered or bottled water. Tap water can often leave an undesirable aftertaste and can even spoil a drink.

balancing your act

Proportion and balance of flavour and texture is at the heart of any cocktail, so accurately measuring your ingredients is of paramount importance. Making cocktails 'by eye' is not recommended. In order to make a perfect cocktail it is best to use a jigger. Ideally a shot is 25ml or one US fluid ounce (29.6 ml). If you buy a measure, it is a good idea to choose one with the quarter and half measure shots indicated on the side.

Apart from the shot, the following common liquid measurements have been used in this book:

dash = ⅓ bar spoon = ½ teaspoon = 2.5 ml

1 teaspoon = 8 dashes = 5 ml

1 tablespoon = 3 teaspoons = ½ fl oz = 15 ml

pinch = the amount of a powdered ingredient that can be held between thumb and forefinger

splash = more than a dash but less than ½ ounce

the basic ingredients

Many would-be cocktail makers are put off by the baffling array of exotic ingredients in some recipes, yet it is a fact that most of the greatest cocktails require just a few basics. It is unnecessary to feel you have to fill your cupboard with strange liqueurs, then watch them sitting there mainly unused for years to come. Many drinks can be made with the following dozen core ingredients:

vodka	gin	rum
bourbon	whisky	cognac
dry vermouth	sweet vermouth	tequila
cointreau	grand marnier	apricot brandy

dressing up for the occasion

A tasteful garnish will make any drink look like a star. The most stylish cocktails are presented with edible garnishes. Avoid the use of garish plastic paraphernalia or paper parasols. Understatement is what you are aiming to achieve. If you are using a wedge of lime or lemon, always use the freshest fruit and make sure it is clean. Rinse olives stored in brine before piercing with a cocktail stick.

making an entrance

Finally, if you are mixing drinks in front of people, remember that the act of preparation itself is an essential part of the fun and enjoyment of cocktails. Don't worry if it all goes wrong. Just relax, sit back and have a drink.

a–z
of
cocktail
recipes

bald eagle shot

½ shot white crème de menthe liqueur
¾ shot tequila

Chill ingredients in the fridge. Layer in a chilled glass by pouring the crème de menthe and carefully pouring the tequila on top.

bee's knees

2 spoons runny honey
1¼ shots light white rum
1¼ shots dark rum
1 shot freshly squeezed orange juice
½ shot double cream
½ shot fresh milk

Stir the rum with the honey until the honey is dissolved, then add the remaining ingredients. Shake with ice and strain into a chilled martini glass.

bee sting

1 spoon runny honey
1 shot whisky
1 shot tequila
2 shots apple juice
top up with ginger ale

Stir the honey with the whisky in the base of the shaker. When the honey is dissolved add the tequila and apple juice. Shake with ice and strain into a tall glass filled with ice. top up with ginger ale.

bald eagle martini

2 shots tequila
1 shot freshly squeezed pink grapefruit juice
½ shot cranberry juice
½ shot freshly squeezed lime juice
½ shot freshly squeezed lemon juice

Shake all ingredients with ice and strain into a chilled martini glass.

bees' knees martini

2 shots gin
4 spoons runny honey
1 shot freshly squeezed orange juice
1 shot freshly squeezed lemon juice

Stir the honey with the gin in the base of a shaker until
the honey is dissolved. Add the lemon and orange juice.
Shake well with ice and then fine strain into a chilled
martini glass.

beetle juice

sprig of fresh mint
1 shot green chartreuse
1 shot vodka
3½ shots apple juice
¼ shots passion fruit sugar syrup

Remove about 8 mint leaves and muddle in the base of
the shaker. Add the remaining ingredients, shake with ice
and strain into an ice-filled glass.

bird of paradise

1¼ shots tequila
3/4 shot white crème de cacao liqueur
½ shot amaretto liqueur
1 shot double cream
¾ shot fresh milk

Add all the ingredients to a shaker. Shake with ice, and strain into a chilled martini glass.

black bison martini

2 shots bison vodka
¼ shot apple schnapps
1¼ shots apple juice
¼ shot dry vermouth

Place the ingredients in a shaker. Shake with ice and pour into a chilled martini glass.

black cat

1 shot vodka
1 shot cherry brandy
3 shots cranberry juice
top up with cola

Shake the vodka, cherry brandy and cranberry juice with ice in a shaker. Pour into an ice-filled glass and top up with the cola.

black mule

2 shots black bottle whisky
handful raspberries
top up with ginger beer

Muddle the raspberries and whisky in the base of the shaker. Shake with ice and pour into an ice-filled glass. top up with the ginger beer.

(Right) In medieval Europe black cats were considered to be wicked. It was said that the devil would borrow the coat of a black cat when he wished to torture his prey. As a result, all-black cats became less common, while those with even a small amount of white fur predominated and even today most black cats have a slight patch of white somewhere.

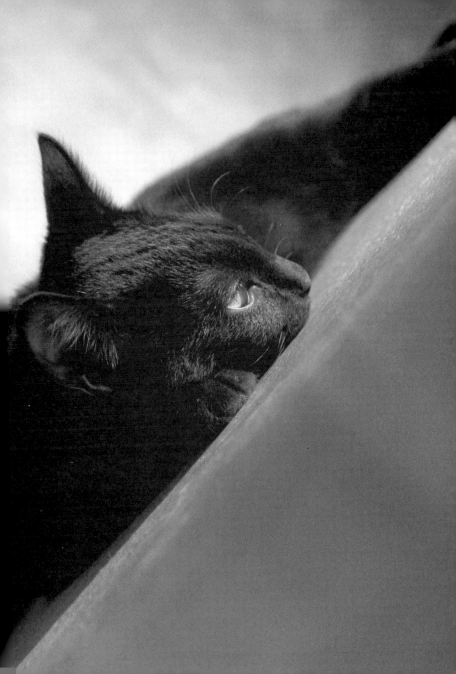

black mussel

½ shot blue curacao liqueur
¼ crème de cassis liqueur
top up with champagne

Pour the liqueurs into a chilled flute glass. top up with champagne.

black widow

1 shot black sambuca
1 shot crème de fraise liqueur
1 shot malibu
½ shot double cream
½ shot fresh milk

Place all the ingredients in an ice filled shaker. Shake well and pour into a chilled martini glass.

bloodhound

2 shots campari
1 shot vodka
4 shots freshly squeezed grapefruit juice

Shake all ingredients with ice. Strain into a tall glass filled with ice.

bluebird

2 shots gin
1 shot blue curacao liqueur
¾ shot freshly squeezed lemon juice
¼ shots almond syrup

Add all the ingredients in a shaker. Shake well with ice and strain into a chilled martini glass.

blue fin

2 shots vodka
1 shot hpnotiq liqueur
1½ shots cranberry juice

Place all the ingredients in a shaker with ice. Shake well and strain into a chilled martini glass.

This recipe originated at the Blue Fin Hotel in Times Square, New York.

blue shark

1 shot tequila
1 shot vodka
½ shot blue curacao liqueur

Place all the ingredients in a shaker with ice. Shake well and strain into a chilled old-fashioned glass filled with ice.

brass monkey

1 shot vodka
½ shot light rum
¼ shot galliano liqueur
2 shots freshly squeezed orange juice

Pour the vodka, rum and orange juice into an ice-filled high ball glass. Stir gently. Float the galliano on top of the drink.

bourbon buck

1 shot vodka
lemon wedge
top up with ginger ale

Squeeze the lemon wedge into an ice-filled highball glass. Add the bourbon, top up with ginger ale, and stir gently.

brazilian mule

2 shots brasilla cachara liqueur
freshly squeezed lime juice
top up with ginger beer

Place all the ingredients in a shaker with ice. Shake well and strain into a chilled glass.

the buck

2½ shots vodka (or other spirit)
½ freshly squeezed lemon juice
top up with ginger ale

Pour the vodka and lemon juice into an ice-filled glass. top up with lemon juice. The Buck was originally created during the Prohibition when it was mixed using gin as a base. A lemon was cut into four pieces and the juice of one of the quarters was squeezed into the drink and the shell dropped into the glass with the juice. If you want to continue the tradition make sure you use an unwaxed lemon.

(Right) During the mating season bucks use their antlers to enter into battle with other males in an attempt to attract a female mate. They begin by circling each other, then bend their legs, lower their head and charge.

bug Juice

2 shots vodka
2 shots freshly squeezed orange juice
top up with pineapple juice

Add all ingredients into a shaker. Shake with ice and strain into an ice-filled glass.

bulldog

1 shot kahlua liqueur
1 shot white rum
2 shots double cream
1 shot milk

Add all ingredients into a shaker. Shake with ice and strain into an ice-filled glass.

bull's kick

2 shots gin
1 shot freshly squeezed lemon juice
½ shot sugar syrup
dash angostura bitters

Shake all ingredients with ice. Strain into a chilled
martini glass.

bull on the loose

2 shots applejack
3 shots chilled apple cider
dash angostura bitters

Shake all ingredients with ice. Strain into a highball glass
filled with ice.

bullfrog

1½ shots vodka
1 shot crème de menthe liqueur
1 shot double cream
1 shot milk

Add all ingredients into a shaker. Shake with ice and
strain into an ice-filled glass.

bull's blood

½ shot white rum
1 shot cognac
1 shot grand marnier
1½ shots freshly squeezed orange juice

Add all ingredients into a shaker. Shake with ice and
strain into a chilled martini glass.

(Right) Bullfrogs have an amazing ability to capture
submerged prey – small turtles, snakes, fish and small insects.
With each leap its eyes remain closed. Finally, with a great
lunge it will bite in using its tiny teeth to hang on.

bull's milk

1 shot dark rum
½ shot cognac
1 teaspoon maple syrup
freshly grated or ground nutmeg
top up with hot milk

Pour the rum and cognac into a heat-resistant mug. Pour in the hot milk, add the maple syrup and stir. Sprinkle the top with nutmeg.

bumble bee

½ shot kahlua liqueur
½ shot sambuca
½ baileys liqueur

Refrigerate ingredients then layer the ingredients, beginning with the kahlua, into a chilled shot glass.

bunny boiler

2 shots pernod
top up with champagne

Pour the pernod into a chilled champagne flute. Slowly top up with the champagne.

bunny hug

2 shots gin
2 shots campari
1 shot sweet vermouth
1 shot freshly squeezed pink grapefruit juice

Shake all ingredients with ice. Strain into a chilled martini glass.

butterfly's kiss

2 shots vodka
1 shot hazelnut liqueur
1 shot cinnamon schnapps
½ shot sugar syrup

Stir ingredients with ice in a shaker. Strain into a chilled martini glass.

buzzard's breath

2½ shots cachaca
1 shot cream of coconut
2 shots pineapple juice
¼ shot double cream
3 tablespoons crushed ice

Add all ingredients into a blender with the ice. Pour into a glass and decorate with pineapple.

(Right) The pure white upper wing surfaces of the Large White are common to both sexes. Although its flight is often hovering or fluttering, this species is a powerful flier and is even migratory in certain years. As with the Small White, often referred to as the Cabbage White, the Large White is mostly to be found near vegetable garden allotments.

canarie

1 shot pastis
1 shot sugar syrup
freshly squeezed lemon juice
top up with chilled mineral water

Pour the pastis, sugar syrup and lemon juice into a chilled glass. Top with mineral water to taste, then finally add the ice to fill the glass.

canaries

1 shot white rum
1 shot cointreau
1 shot crème de bananes liqueur
1 shot cherry brandy liqueur
2 shots pineapple juice
3 shots freshly squeezed orange juice

Add all ingredients to a shaker. Shake with ice and strain into a glass filled with ice.

canary flip

2 shots dry white wine
2 shots advocaat
1 shot freshly squeezed lemon juice

Add all ingredients to a shaker. Shake with ice and strain into a chilled martini glass.

cheeky cow

2 shots brandy
1 shot ruby port
½ shot cointreau

Stir all ingredients in an ice-filled glass, then strain into a chilled martini glass.

cheeky monkey

1 shot lemon vodka
1 shot yellow chartreuse
2 shots freshly squeezed orange juice
½ shot sugar syrup
dash orange bitters

Add all ingredients to a shaker. Shake with ice and strain
into a chilled martini glass.

(Right) Chimpanzees split from human evolution roughly six
million years ago and the chimpanzee remains our closest
relative in the animal kingdom. Chimpanzees are highly
sophisticated and intelligent. They not only make tools and use
them to acquire food and for social displays, but are conscious
of status and can understand various aspects of human
language. They also have complex hunting strategies, but what
sets them apart is their ability to engage in altruistic behaviour
towards others in their group. There is evidence of emotional
awarenes, some chimpanzees having shown displays of
mourning, empathy, respect towards other species and strong
emotional bonding with other chimpanzees and humans.

cicada

2 shots whisky
1 shot amaretto liqueur
½ shot double cream
1 shot sugar syrup

Add all ingredients to a shaker. Shake with ice and strain into a chilled martini glass.

crouching tiger

1 shot tequila
1 shot passion fruit liqueur

Add both ingredients to a shaker. Shake with ice and strain into a chilled shot glass.

(Right) The white tiger, also known as the Bengal tiger, is one of the world's most endangered species, hunted by poachers in many Asian countries to the point of near extinction. It is about 3 metres long and weighs anything from 400 to about 570 pounds. The white fur is caused by a recessive gene. Although slow runners white tigers are stealthy enough to make them fearsome predators.

crown stag

2 shots vodka
2 shots jagermeister liqueur
1 shot raspberry crème de menthe

Add all ingredients to a shaker. Shake with ice and strain into a chilled shot glass.

dead man's mule

1 shot absinthe
1 shot cinnamon schnapps liqueur
1 shot almond syrup
½ shot freshly squeezed lime juice
top up with ginger beer

Add the absinthe, cinnamon schnapps, almond syrup and lime juice to a shaker. Shake with ice and strain into a chilled glass. Finally top up with the ginger beer.

(Left) With the exception of the Chinese water deer, which possesses tusks, all deer have antlers. Each species of deer has its own antler structure. Fallow deer and moose antlers have a broad central stalk, whereas mule deer and white-tailed varieties have two bifurcated, or branched antlers, where the main stem divides into two, each of which divides again.

diamond dog

1 shot campari
1 shot dry vermouth
1 shot rose's lime cordial
1 shot freshly squeezed orange juice

Add all ingredients to a shaker. Shake with ice and strain into an ice-filled glass.

dog's nose

1 shot gin
top up with chilled ale

Slowly pour the ale into a chilled beer mug. Pour the gin into the mug of beer. Alternatively pour the gin into a chilled shot glass and drop in to the mug of beer.

(Right) A dog's nose is highly sensitive. The olfactory bulb in a dog's brain is relatively about forty times larger than in humans, with 125 to 220 million smell-sensitive receptors. Dogs can discriminate odours at concentrations almost 100 million times lower than humans are able to do. A wet nose is essential for determining the direction of the air current in which the scent is held.

dragonfly

1 shot gin
lime wedge
top up with ginger ale

Pour the gin into an ice-filled old-fashioned glass. Top with the ginger ale and stir gently. Squeeze the lime wedge over the drink, and drop it in.

fat mule

1 shot tia maria liqueur
4 shots guinness, refrigerated
top up with cola

Pour the tia maria and guinness into an ice-filled glass. top up with cola.

(Previous page) Dalmations are loyal and active dogs, revered for their excellent memories. They should be handled and socialized from a young age to prevent timidity and aggression as a result of fear.

flipper

2 shots freshly squeezed lemon juice
½ shot cointreau
top up with champagne

Pour the lemon juice and cointreau into a chilled champagne flute. Top up with champagne.

fish house punch

1 shot cognac
1 shot golden rum
¾ shot peach brandy (or peach schnapps liqueur)
¾ shot freshly squeezed lemon juice
¼ shot sugar syrup
2 shots chilled mineral water

Add all ingredients to a shaker. Shake with ice and strain into an ice-filled glass.

The recipe for this well known punch dates back as far as 1732 to a social club in Philadelphia called State in Schuylkill, where the drink was mixed in volume and served out of a great glass bowl. Over the years the recipe has been adapted and modernised. It is argued that the original recipe omitted the peach brandy altogether and some versions use soda water instead of mineral water.

flamingo

1 shot bourbon
1 shot crème de bananes liqueur
½ shot freshly squeezed lemon juice
2 shots freshly squeezed orange juice
½ fresh egg white

Add all ingredients to a shaker. Shake with ice and strain into a chilled martini glass.

flutter

2 shots tequila
1 shot tequila liqueur
1 shot pineapple juice

Add all ingredients to a shaker. Shake with ice and strain into a chilled martini glass.

(Right) Different species of flamingo have different shades of pink feathers. A Caribbean flamingo has the most coloration, whereas the feathers Chilean flamingo are extremely pale. A flamingo's pink feather colour comes from its diet of diatoms, seeds, algae, crustaceans and mollusks which they filter through the water.

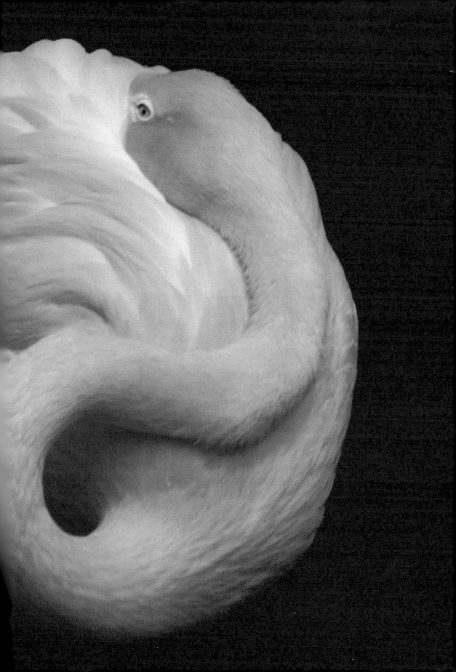

fluffy duck

1½ shots gin
1 shot advocaat liqueur
½ shot cointreau
1 shot freshly squeezed orange juice
top up with soda water

Shake the gin, advocaat, cointreau and orange juice with ice. Strain into an ice-filled glass and top up with the soda.

flying grasshopper

1 shot vodka
1 shot white crème de cacao liqueur
½ shot white crème de menthe liqueur
¾ shot double cream
¾ shot fresh milk

Add all ingredients to a shaker. Shake with ice and strain into a chilled martini glass.

(Right) A chick begins to hatch by 'pipping', pecking a breathing hole with its egg tooth towards the blunt end of the egg. It will rest for some hours, absorbing the remaining egg yolk and withdrawing the blood supply from the membrane beneath the shell. It then enlarges the hole, turning round as it goes, and eventually severing the blunt end of the shell to make a lid. As it crawls out, its wet down dries out in the warmth of the nest.

flying tiger

2 shots white rum
1 shot gin
¼ shot sugar syrup
¼ shot grenadine
3 dashes angostura bitters
1 shot chilled mineral water

Add all ingredients to a shaker. Shake with ice and strain into a chilled martini glass.

It is believed that the recipe for Flying Tiger was devised by a captain serving in the US marines during the Second World War at Santiago de Cuba. It was subsequently published in Esquire's Handbook for Hosts in 1949.

french mule

2 shots cognac
1 shot sugar syrup
3 dashes angostura bitters
1 shot freshly squeezed lime juice
top up with ginger beer

Shake the cognac, lime juice, sugar syrup and angostura bitters with ice. Strain into an ice-filled glass. top up with ginger beer.

frisky bison

2 shots bison vodka
½ shots dry vermouth
top up with lemonade

Pour into a long glass filled with ice and stir.

frit fly

1 shot tequila
1 shot vodka
1 shot kahlua

Shake ingredients with ice. Strain into a chilled glass.

(Overleaf) Spider monkeys live in evergreen rainforests, semi-deciduous and mangrove forests, almost never coming to the ground and living mostly in the upper canopy. Spider monkeys are known for their long, muscular tails which they use as an extra limb when climbing and swinging through the trees, leaving the hands free to gather food. Acrobatic and agile, the monkeys can move in this way with one arm slide reaching as far as forty feet. Tragically there has been a continuing decline in its habitat due to the destruction of the rainforest and the spider monkey is now an endangered species due to the fact that it lives only in severely fragmented populations.

funky monkey

1 shot golden rum
1 shot crème de cacao liqueur
1 shot crème de bananes liqueur
1 shot cream of coconut
1 shot cream 1 shot milk
1 small banana, peeled
3 tablespoons crushed ice

Blend all ingredients in a blender and pour into a goblet.

fuzzy penguin

1 shot cointreau
1 shot tequila
1 shot spiced rum
3 shots pineapple juice

Add all ingredients to a shaker. Shake with ice and strain into a chilled glass.

(Overleaf) A fine down covers most newly hatched penguin chicks, including these emperor chicks. The down feathers are not waterproof, so they must stay out of the water until they require their juvenile plumage. Huddling together in subzero temperatures these emperor penguins are left in a kindergarten group dependent on their attentive parents for survival during the short Arctic summer.

game bird

2 shots scotch whisky
½ shot elderflower cordial
1 shot sour apple liqueur
½ shot sugar syrup
½ shot freshly squeezed lemon juice
top up with ginger ale

Shake the first five ingredients with ice and strain into a glass filled with ice. Top up with ginger ale.

gin gin mule

2 shots gin
½ shot freshly squeezed lime juice
¼ shot sugar syrup
2 small slices fresh root ginger
3 dashes angostura bitters
top up with ginger beer

Muddle the ginger in the base of a shaker. Add the gin, lime juice, the sugar syrup and the angostura bitters. Top up with ginger beer.

(Right) Donkeys have developed loud vocalizations, which help them to keep in contact with other donkeys over long distances of the desert and their larger ears are thought to pick up distant sounds.

ginger tom

2 shots gin
1 shot freshly squeezed lemon juice
½ shot sugar syrup
2 small slices fresh root ginger
top up with soda water

Muddle the ginger in the base of a shaker. Add the other ingredients. Shake with ice and strain into a tall glass filled with ice.

golden bird

1 shot grand marnier
1 shot light rum
½ shot crème de bananes liqueur
2 shots freshly squeezed orange juice
1 shot pineapple juice

Add all ingredients to a shaker. Shake with ice and strain into a chilled martini glass.

golden dragon

2 shots tequila
½ shot pison amber liqueur
1 shot freshly squeezed lime juice
2 shots apple juice
½ shots passion fruit sugar syrup

Add all ingredients to a shaker. Shake with ice and strain into a glass filled with ice.

golden goose

2 shots gin
½ shot freshly squeezed lemon juice
½ shot sugar syrup
1 fresh egg yolk
top up with club soda

Shake the gin, lemon juice, egg yolk and sugar syrup with ice. Strain into an ice-filled highball glass. Top up with club soda and stir gently.

golden retriever

1 shot white rum
1 shot green chartreuse
1 shot cuarenta y très liqueur
1 shot chilled mineral water

Stir all ingredients with ice and strain into a glass filled
with ice.

The aimiable, kindly and confident nature of golden retrievers is a hallmark of the breed. A typical golden retriever will be calm, intelligent, biddable and friendly with those they know as well as strangers. They also have an exceptional eagerness to please. Unsurprisingly, their gentle, trusting disposition makes them poor guard dogs.

gorilla

1 shot dark rum
1 shot bourbon
½ shot kalhua liqueur

Shake the ingredients with ice. Strain into an ice-filled old-fashioned glass.

(Right) A fully grown male gorilla is over 1.5 metres tall and weighs about 180 kilos. Yet, despite being the biggest and strongest apes on the planet, gorillas are in fact shy and gentle creatures. As leaf-eaters, they require vast quantities of vegetation just to survive, and so it is hardly surprising that feeding takes up a great deal of their time. On average gorillas will spend six hours a day picking and chewing their food.

A family group – typically one alpha male, a harem of several adult females and about half a dozen young – might travel around half a mile each day seeking out the best leaves and stems, finally resting wherever they find themselves in fresh new beds. As trees are felled for timber and the landscape cleared for crops and cattle, the forests of these maginificent animals are continually in decline. Unless we can find a way to help them, these intelligent and beautiful animals are in danger of being lost altogether.

green eyes

2 shots vodka
½ shot blue curacao liqueur
1 shot freshly squeezed orange juice
½ shot freshly squeezed lemon juice
¼ shot almond syrup

Add all ingredients to a shaker. Shake with ice and strain into a chilled martini glass.

greenfly

½ shot melon liqueur
½ shot crème de menthe liqueur
½ shot green chartreuse

Refrigerate ingredients before layering into a chilled glass.

green lizard

½ shot green chartreuse
½ shot rum

Pour the chartreuse into a chilled shot glass. Float the rum on top and down in one.

green spider

1 shot vodka
½ shot peppermint syrup
2 shots tonic water
sprig fresh mint

Shake the vodka, syrup and tonic with ice. Strain into a chilled martini glass and garnish with the mint sprig.

greyhound

2 shots vodka
top up with freshly squeezed pink grapefruit juice

Add all ingredients to a shaker. Shake with ice and strain into a chilled glass filled with ice.

grey mouse

1 shot baileys liqueur
½ shot black sambuca

Shake both ingredients with ice then strain into a chilled shot glass.

(Right) From the Anglo-Norman 'dormeus' meaning 'sleepy one', it is not surprising that one of the most notable characteristics of dormice living in temperate climates is hibernation. Dormice can hibernate for six months a year and even longer, sometimes waking for only brief eriods to eat food previously stored nearby. The common dormouse is no longer common, but in serious decline due to loss of ancient woodland and hedges resulting in fragmentation of habitats, isolation of dormouse populations and local extinctions.

grizzly bear

1 shot gin
1 shot kahlua
1 shot fresh double cream.

Shake all ingredients with ice and strain into a chilled martini glass.

hair of the dog

3 spoons runny honey
2 shots scotch whisky
1 shot double cream
1 shot milk

Stir the honey with the whisky until the honey dissolves. Add the remaining ingredients, shake with ice and strain into a chilled glass.

(Left) The diet of the Alaskan brown bear is mainly vegetarian, especially fruits, roots and berries, but when the opportunity presents itself, meat or fish is a rare treat. Once a year the migration of salmon to their spawning grounds up river offers the bear a great feast. Fish are caught in the water, carried to the riverbank and the flesh separated from the skeleton.

honey bee

2 shots white rum
2 spoons runny honey
½ shot freshly squeezed lemon juice
1 shot chilled mineral water

Stir the honey with the vodka in the base of a shaker until the honey is dissolved. Add the remaining ingredients. Shake with ice and strain into a chilled martini glass.

hop toad

1½ shot white rum
1 shot apricot brandy
1 shot freshly squeezed lime juice
½ shot chilled mineral water

Add all ingredients to a shaker. Shake with ice and strain into a chilled martini glass.

hopping hound

1 shot brandy
1 shot fernet branca
1 shot white creme de menthe

Stir the ingredients in a mixing glass with ice. Strain into a chilled martini glass.

horsefly

2 shots sloe gin
1 shot sweet vermouth

Stir the ingredients in a mixing glass with ice. Strain into a chilled martini glass.

horse's neck

2 shots bourbon
1 ounce benedictine liqueur
2 dashes angostura bitters
top up with ginger ale

Coat the chilled highball glass with bitters. Fill the glass with ice, pour in the bourbon and Benedictine. top up with the ginger ale and stir gently.

horse's neck with a kick

2 shots bourbon
3 dashes angostura bitters
top up with ginger ale

Pour ingredients into a tall glass filled with ice and stir.

(Right) There is often confusion regarding what actually makes a white horse. True white horses have unpigmented pink skin and unpigmented white hair, although eye colour varies. Gray horses have a white-like coat colour, but most have black skin and dark eyes. Gray foals may be born any colour, but the coloured hairs of their coat become progressively silvered as they age, eventually resulting in a white or near-white coat as they reach maturity. Many famous horses are actually grays with their coats turned fully white.

iguana

½ shot vodka
½ shot tequila
½ shot kahlua liqueur

Add all ingredients to a shaker. Shake with ice and strain into a chilled shot glass.

iguana wana

1 shot vodka
1 shot peach schnapps liqueur
3 shots freshly squeezed orange juice

Shake all ingredients with ice and strain into a tall glass filled with ice.

(Left) Iguanas have superb vision and can see long distances in great detail, relying on their eyes to navigate through trees, find food and to communicate with other iguanas. All iguanas also possess a third eye, known as a palietal eye which appears as a pale scale on the top of the head and a large, round, distinctive scale on the cheek, known as a subtympanic shield. This is also highly sensitive, as is the ear which lies above the shield and behind the eye.

irish buck

1 shot Irish whisky
top up with ginger ale
lemon wedge

Squeeze the lemon wedge into an ice-filled highball glass.
Add the whisky, top up with ginger ale, and stir gently.

jamaican mule

2 shots spiced rum
½ shot freshly squeezed lime juice
½ shot sugar syrup
top up with ginger beer

Pour ingredients into a tall glass filled with ice.
Stir gently.

jungle bird

½ shot campari
½ shot white rum
½ shot freshly squeezed lime juice
½ shot sugar syrup
2 shots pineapple juice

Add all ingredients to a shaker. Shake with ice and strain into an ice-filled glass.

jungle juice

1 shot vodka
2 shot white rum
½ shot cointreau
1 shot freshly squeezed orange juice
1 shot freshly squeezed lime juice
1 shot pineapple juice
1 shot cranberry juice

Shake all the ingredients with ice. Strain into a tall glass filled with ice.

leap frog

1½ shots gin
½ shot freshly squeezed lemon juice
lime wedge
top up with chilled ginger ale

Pour the gin and lemon juice into an ice-filled old-fashioned glass. top up with the ginger ale and stir gently. Squeeze the lime wedge over the drink and drop it in.

limey mule

2 shots vodka
1 shot freshly squeezed lime juice
½ shot sugar syrup
top up with ginger ale

Shake the vodka, lime juice and sugar syrup with ice and strain into an ice-filled glass. top up with ginger ale.

(Right) The red-eyed tree frog has three eyelids and sticky pads on its toes. During the mating season male frogs shake the branches they are sitting on in order to improve their chances of finding a mate by keeping their rivals at bay. When the rainfall is at its peak, they then call out to attract the attention of the female. If successful, she will carry the male around for several hours during the oviposition process.

lonely bull

2 shots tequila
2 shots kahlua liqueur
1 shot double cream
1 shot milk

Add all ingredients to a shaker. Shake with ice and strain into a glass filled with ice.

lovely butterfly

1½ shots dry vermouth
1½ shots sweet vermouth
1 shot dubonnet red
1 shot freshly squeezed orange juice

Add all ingredients to a shaker. Shake with ice and strain into a chilled martini glass.

mad dog

1 shot vodka
¼ shot blackcurrant cordial
dash tabasco

Pour the vodka into a chilled shot glass. Layer the blackcurrant on top and add a dash of Tabasco.

mat the rat

2 shots spiced rum
½ shot cointreau
2 shots freshly squeezed orange juice
½ shot freshly squeezed lime juice
top up with lemonade

Shake the rum, cointreau, orange juice and lime juice with ice and strain into an ice-filled glass.

mezcal buck

1 shot mezcal
lemon wedge
top up with ginger ale

Squeeze the lemon wedge into an ice-filled highball glass.
Add the mezcal, top up with ginger ale, and stir gently.

mexican mule

2 shots tequila
1 shot freshly squeezed lime juice
½ shot sugar syrup
top up with ginger beer

Shake the tequila, lime juice and sugar syrup with ice.
Strain into an ice-filled glass.

mongoose's blush

1 shot brandy
2 shots pink grapefruit juice
2 shots apricot juice
dash grenadine

Shake all ingredients with ice. Strain into a chilled martini glass.

monkey hop

1 shot crème de cassis
½ shot freshly squeezed lemon juice
½ shot Kirsch
top up with soda water

Shake the kirsch, crème de cassis and lemon juice with ice. Strain into an ice-filled glass and top up with the soda.

monkey gland

2 shots gin
¼ shot absinthe
1½ shots freshly squeezed orange juice
¼ shot grenadine

Add all ingredients to a shaker. Shake with ice and strain into a glass filled with ice.

monkey shine

2 shots golden rum
1 shot malibu liqueur
1 shot pineapple juice

Add all ingredients to a shaker. Shake with ice and strain into a chilled martini glass.

monkey wrench

2 shots golden rum
top up with freshly squeezed grapefruit juice

Pour the rum into a glass filled with ice. top up with the grapefruit juice and stir gently.

moscow mule

1 shot vodka
½ shot freshly squeezed lime juice
¼ shot sugar syrup
2 dashes angostura bitters
lime wedge
top up with ginger beer

Shake the vodka, lime juice and sugar syrup with ice and strain into an ice-filled glass. top up with ginger beer and garnish with a lime wedge.

The classic combination of vodka and ginger beer was the brain child of two men over a drink at New York's Chatham Bar in 1941. Jack Morgan was launching his own ginger beer, while John G. Martin had bought the trademark brand of Smirnoff Vodka for a small distribution company in Conneticut named Hublein.

In deciding to combine forces and mix the two ingredients together, they created a lasting cocktail great. The drink was initially advertised with a promotional gimic, when special Moscow Mule mugs engraved with a kicking mule were sold alongside the Vodka. If you can find one nowadays, they are a collector's item.

mule's hind leg

1 shot gin
1 shot benedictine
1 shot Calvados
1 shot apricot brandy
½ shot chilled mineral water.

Add all ingredients to a shaker. Shake with ice and strain into a chilled martini glass.

new orleans mule

2 shots bourbon
1 shot kahlua liqueur
1 shot pineapple juice
½ shot lime juice
top up with ginger beer

Shake the bourbon, kahlua, pineapple juice and lime juice with ice. Strain into a glass filled with ice and top up with the ginger beer.

newt's tongue

2 shot campari
1 sugar cube
2 dashes angostura bitters
lemon peel
top up with chilled champagne

Run the lemon peel around the rim of a chilled flute glass. Soak the sugar cube in the bitters. Pour in the brandy and top up with champagne.

old bird

1 shot brandy
1 shot cointreau
½ shot freshly squeezed lemon juice
½ shot sugar syrup

Shake the ingredients with ice and strain into a chilled martini glass.

orang-a-tang

1½ shots vodka
½ shot rum
1 shot cointreau
2 shots freshly squeezed orange juice
½ shot freshly squeezed lime juice
¼ shot grenadine

Shake the vodka, cointreau, orange juice, lime juice and grenadine with ice. Strain into a glass filled with ice. Float the rum on top of the drink.

(Right) The people of Indonesia and Malaysia call the orangutan 'orang hutan', which translates as 'people of the forest'. In the past they would not kill them because they were like people hiding in the trees. Orangutans are extremely intelligent and have been known to use leaves as umbrellas to protect from the rain or as cups to drink water. They are shy and solitary. The males and females stay together for just a few days during mating, and it is the females who then look after their offspring. Never before has their livelihood been so severely threatened. Economic crisis combined with natural disasters and human abuse of the forest are pushing this beautiful animal to the point of extinction. In the last twenty years eighty per cent of their habitat has been lost.

owl

2 shots gin
1 shot white crème de cacao liqueur
1 egg white
dash grenadine

Shake the gin, egg white and crème de cacao with ice. Strain into a chilled martini glass. Make two drops in the centre of the drink with the grenadine. Do not stir.

panther's claw

2 shots gin
2 teaspoons sweet vermouth
½ shot black sambuca

Shake all ingredients with ice and strain into a chilled martini glass.

(Left) This snowy owl is a powerful bird. With a wingspan of some 150 cms and a sharp black bill it is no wonder it has few predators in the wild, perfectly adapted for life north of the arctic circle, where it feeds mainly on lemmings and other rodents or, at times of low prey density, young ptarmigan and even fish. This adult male is virtually pure white, whereas the females and younger birds have dark scalloping.

panda martini

1 shot vodka
½ shot dark crème de cacao liqueur
½ shot white crème de cacao liqueur
½ shot kirsch liqueur
dark chocolate shavings
cherry, stemmed and stoned

Rim a chilled martini glass with icing sugar and place the cherry at the bottom of the glass. Shake the dark crème de cacao, vodka and kirsch with ice and pour into the glass. Gently layer the white crème de cacao on top and sprinkle the chocolate shavings over the top.

(Right) Like the polar bear, the panda is under serious threat of extinction and it will die out if the forests of bamboo upon which it depends continue disappear. Giant pandas are well known to be amongst the most discerning of animals as well as the most adored. By and large they live alone, and the females have a territory which they defend fiercely against other females. They are also extremely fussy eaters. Their daily diet consists of around 20 to 30 pounds of bamboo, and although there are 200 varieties, they will only eat twenty of those.

pink flamingo

2 shots orange vodka
1 shot freshly squeezed orange juice
1 shot cranberry juice

Add all ingredients to a shaker. Shake with ice and strain into a glass filled with ice.

pink hound

2 shots gin
1½ shots pink grapefruit juice
½ shot sugar syrup

Add all ingredients to a shaker. Shake with ice and strain into a chilled martini glass.

potted parrot

2 shots white rum
1 shot cointreau
2 shots freshly squeezed orange juice
1 shot freshly squeezed lemon juice
¼ shot sugar syrup

Add all ingredients to a shaker. Shake with ice and strain into a glass filled with ice.

pony on the run

1 shot gin
½ shot freshly squeezed lemon juice
Top up with champagne

Shake the gin and lemon juice with ice. Strain into a chilled martini glass. Top up slowly with champagne and stir slowly.

polar bear

1 shot mint schnapps
1 shot crème de cacao

Layer ingredients in a chilled shot glass.

pink polar bear

2 shots vodka
1 shot tia maria
1 shot grenadine
top up with fresh milk, chilled

Shake the vodka, tia maria and grenadine with ice. Strain into an ice-filled glass and top up with the milk.

(Left) The polar bear is well known to be under serious threat of extinction from global warming due to the melting of its sea-ice habitat. At present these beautiful creatures are the largest living land carnivores in the world. An adult male can weigh up to 1300 pounds, though the cubs when born are no bigger than a rat. The fur of a polar bear appears white to the naked eye because of the reflected wavelengths of light, but the long, coarse guard hairs that protect the thick undercoat are actually hollow and transparent. A thick layer of blubber provides excellent insulation against the harsh arctic winter and furred feet have good traction on the ice.

prairie oyster

1 shot cognac
1 egg yolk
1 barspoon malt vinegar
2 dashes of tabasco sauce
1 barspoon worcestershire sauce
salt and pepper

Place the egg yolk, unbroken into a margarita glass. Gently pour in the rest of the ingredients without breaking the yolk. Drink it down in one – and pray.

The prairie oyster is a regular remedy that will be offered by most barmen. It tastes as unpleasant as one of the stories about the origin of its name. 'Prairie oysters' in the cattle-raising areas of the United States was the local term for calves' testicles, after the cattle had been castrated and their redundant organs had been fried for breakfast. Whether the breakfast dish was named after the drink or the drink after the dish is uncertain. There is no doubt that the egg floating in the glass does look like a disembodied eyeball. Not one for the squeamish!

(Right) Prairie dogs are in fact a type of ground squirrel, named after their habitat and their call, which sounds like a dog's bark. They are highly social animals, and live in large families and collections of families known as towns that can span hundreds of acres.

pussyfoot

4 shots freshly squeezed orange juice
½ shot freshly squeezed lemon juice
½ shot freshly squeezed lime juice
dash grenadine
stemmed cherry

Shake all of the ingredients in a cocktail shaker filled with ice. Strain into a rocks glass. Garnish with a stemmed cherry.

Kittens develop very quickly from about two weeks of age until their seventh week. Their co-ordination and strength improve, they learn to wash themselves, play-fight with each other, releasing their natural hunting and stalking instincts.

playmate martini

1 shot cognac
1 shot apricot brandy
1 shot grand marnier
1 shot freshly squeezed orange juice
2 dashes angostura bitters

Add all ingredients to a shaker. Shake with ice and strain into a chilled martini glass.

raspberry mule

2 shots vodka
1 shot freshly squeezed lime juice
½ shot sugar syrup
handful fresh raspberries

Muddle the raspberries in the base of a shaker. Add the lime juice, vodka and sugar syrup and shake with ice. Strain into a glass filled with ice and top up with ginger beer. Stir gently.

rat pack manhattan

1 shot bourbon
1 shot grand marnier
1 shot sweet vermouth
1 shot dry vermouth
dash angostura bitters

Pour grand marnier into a chilled martini glass then discard the liquid. Stir the other ingredients with ice and strain into the coated glass.

raging bull

½ shot sambuca
½ shot kahlua liqueur
½ shot tequila

Chill the ingredients in the fridge, then layer in a chilled shot glass beginning with the Sambuca.

rattlesnake

2 shots Bourbon
½ shot freshly squeezed lemon juice
½ shot sugar syrup
½ fresh egg white
1 shot chilled mineral water
dash absinthe

Shake all ingredients with ice and strain into a chilled martini glass. Harry Craddock said of this cocktail 'It will either cure a rattlesnake bite, or kill rattlesnakes, or make you see them.'

red breast

2 shots whisky
½ shot freshly squeezed lime juice
2 dashes grenadine
top up with ginger beer

Pour the whisky, lime juice and ginger beer into a rocks glass filled with ice. Drizzle the Grenadine on the surface of the drink.

(Left) The robin was originally called the 'redbreast' because of the distinctive orange breast of both sexes of robin, since 'orange' as the name of a colour was unknown in English until the sixteenth century. Often confused in its lyrical song with the nightingale a robin sings to defend its territory, often in the evening and into the night during the autumn and winter. Around Christmas it will begin exploring the territories of other robins to seek a mate. By mid-January most robins will be paired at which point the females will stop singing, although their male partners continue to sing to declare their joint breeding territory.

red lion

2 shots gin
¼ shot grand marnier
½ shot freshly squeezed lime juice
¼ shot grenadine

Add all ingredients to a shaker. Shake with ice and strain into a chilled martini glass.

(Right) The average gestation period for a lion cub is around 110 days, the female giving birth to a litter of one to four cubs in a secluded den usually away from the rest of the pride. A lioness will often hunt by herself whilst the cubs are still helpless, staying relatively close to the thicket or den where the cubs are kept. Lion cubs are born blind and and almost helpless, beginning to crawl a day or two after birth. Their eyes do not open until roughly a week after birth and it is around three weeks of age before they are walking and playing. During this stage they are highly vulnerable, facing predation by jackals, hyenas, leopards, martial eagles, snakes and even buffaloes.

red panda

2 shots gin
1 shot freshly squeezed lemon juice
2 dashes grenadine
1 dash ruby port

Shake the gin, lemon juice and grenadine with ice. Strain into a martini glass and gently float the port on top.

white rhino

2 shots lillet blanc
top up with 2 ounches chilled soda

Pour the lillet over a few ice cubes in a chilled glass. Add the soda and stir.

(Left) Red pandas come from forests in the foothills of the Himalayas, where their thick red fur keeps them warm in the harsh temperatures and provides good camouflage in trees often covered with reddish lichen. They are superb climbers, using their long tail for balance and a 'super thumb' for hanging onto the branches. Like the giant panda, red pandas eat bamboo, although in other respects scientists argue over whether red pandas are in fact more closely related to raccoons.

red snapper

3 shots tomato juice
dash freshly squeezed lemon juice
1 shot gin
pinch celery salt
2 dashes worcestershire sauce
2 dashes tabasco sauce
freshly ground black pepper

Fill a highball glass with ice-cubes, then pour in the tomato and lemon juices. Add the gin, celery salt and sauces and stir. Add a quick twist of black pepper. Garnish with a wedge of lime on the rim, and a stalk of celery, if requested. Serve with a stirrer.

reed warbler's revenge

2 shots golden rum
3 shots cranberry juice
1 shot pineapple juice

Put the ingredients into an ice-filled highball glass and stir gently.

reef juice

2 shots gin
4 shots tomato juice
½ shot freshly squeezed lemon juice
3 dashes worcestershire sauce
5 drops tabasco sauce
½ shot port
pinch celery salt
pinch freshly ground black pepper

Add all ingredients to a shaker. Shake with ice and strain into a glass filled with ice.

remember the mane

2 shots bourbon
1 shot absinthe
½ shot cherry brandy
½ shot sweet vermouth
top up with chilled mineral water

Pour the absinthe into a glass filled with ice and top up with water. Pour the whisky, cherry brandy and vermouth into a second glass filled with ice and stir gently. Discard the absinthe and ice from the first glass, then strain the contents of the second into the first.

roadrunner

2 shots tequila
1 shot freshly squeezed lemon juice
½ shot sugar syrup
dash angostura bitters

Add all ingredients to a shaker. Shake with ice and strain into a chilled martini glass.

rum buck

1 shot rum
top up with ginger ale

Squeeze the lemon wedge into an ice-filled highball glass. Add the rum, top up with ginger ale, and stir gently.

salty dog

2 shots vodka
2 shots freshly squeezed grapefruit juice
¼ shot sugar syrup
salt

Wet the rim of a chilled martini glass and press into salt. Once the rim has been coated, shake the remaining ingredients with ice and strain into the glass.

satan's whiskers

1 shot gin
1 shot dry vermouth
1 shot sweet vermouth
½ shot grand marnier
1 shot freshly squeezed orange juice
dash orange bitters

Add all ingredients to a shaker. Shake with ice and strain into a chilled martini glass.

scorpion

2 shots white rum
1 shot cognac
2 shots freshly squeezed orange juice
1 shot freshly squeezed lemon juice
½ shot sugar syrup
handful crushed ice

Blend ingredients and pour into a chilled glass.

scotch buck

1 shot scotch whisky
lemon wedge
top up with ginger ale

Squeeze the lemon wedge into an ice-filled highball glass.
Add the whisky, top up with ginger ale, and stir gently.

shark bite

2 shots rum
3 shots freshly squeezed orange juice
½ shot freshly squeezed lemon juice
1 shot grenadine
handful crushed ice

Blend the rum, orange juice and lime juice with the crushed ice and pour into a glass. Drizzle the Grenadine around the edge.

snakebite

¼ pint lager
¼ pint cider

Pour lager into a tall glass. Top up with the cider.

snoopy

1½ shots bourbon
1 shot galliano
1 shot grand marnier
½ shot campari
¼ shot freshly squeezed lemon juice

Add all ingredients to a shaker. Shake with ice and strain
into a glass filled with ice.

sourpuss martini

1 shot lemon vodka
½ shot melon liqueur
½ shot sour apple liqueur
2 shots apple juice

Add all ingredients to a shaker. Shake with ice and strain
into a chilled martini glass.

southern mule

2 shots southern comfort
½ shot freshly squeezed lime juice
top up with ginger beer

Shake the lime juice and southern comfort with ice and strain into a glass filled with ice. top up with ginger beer and stir gently.

spanish fly

1½ shots mezcal
1 shot grand marnier
pinch instant coffee

Pour the mezcal and grand marnier into an ice-filled old-fashioned glass. Sprinkle the coffee on the top.

spikey hedgehog

1 shot cranberry juice
1 shot grenadine
dash freshly squeezed lime juice
top up with soda water

Shake the cranberry juice, grenadine and lime with ice. Pour the ingredients into an ice-filled highball glass and top up with the soda.

squashed frog

½ shot melon liqueur
½ shot advocaat
½ shot grenadine

Refrigerate ingredients until chilled. Layer in a chilled shot glass.

(Left) There are many hazards facing hedgehogs in today's world – cars, lawnmowers, litter – but the greatest of all is their loss of habitat due to changes in farming practises. The preference for large fields over smaller ones have meant that many hedgehog-friendly hedges and vegetated areas are in decline. There are nowadays far fewer places for a hedgehog to root about in the undergrowth in search of the small creatures that compose their diet.

stork club

1 shot gin
1 shot cointreau
1 shot freshly squeezed orange juice
½ shot freshly squeezed lime juice

Add all ingredients to a shaker. Shake with ice and strain into a chilled martini glass.

(Right) The white stork is a huge bird, up to 125 cms tall, with a wingspan of up to 200 cms. Their nests are equally large, and are famously built up high on trees, buildings and special platforms. Like swans, storks were previously thought to be monogamous, though recent research has shown that they do change partners and are often as much attached to a nest as another stork.

the swan

1 shot gin
1 shot dry vermouth
1 shot freshly squeezed lime juice
4 dashes pastis
1 dash abbott's bitters

Shake the ingredients in a shaker with ice. Strain into a chilled martini glass.

tennessee berry mule

1½ shots tennessee whisky
1 shot amaretto liqueur
1 shot cranberry juice
12 raspberries
top up with ginger beer

Muddle the raspberries in the base of a shaker. Add the whisky, Amaretto and cranberry juice. Shake with ice and strain into a glass filled with ice. Top up with ginger beer and stir gently.

(Right) The name 'swan' is derived from the Indo-European stem 'swen', meaning 'to sound' or 'to sing'. Swans are famous for their ability to form monogamous pair bonds, often mating for life. However, research has shown that some pairings result in separation owing sometimes to breeding difficulties.

tequila mockingbird

2 shots tequila
½ shot crème de menthe
½ shot freshly squeezed lemon juice
½ shot chilled mineral water

Add all ingredients to a shaker. Shake with ice and strain into a chilled martini glass.

thunderbird

1 shot bourbon
1 shot pineapple juice
1 shot freshly squeezed orange juice

Add all ingredients to a shaker. Shake with ice and strain into a chilled martini glass.

(Right) Hummingbirds are the only birds who can fly backwards and have the highest matabolism of all animals. By rapidly flapping their wings up to ninety times a second they can also hover in the hair with great precision whilst feeding on nectar with their long beaks. In this way they perform an essential role in pollen transfer between flowers. They can also fly at high speeds, sometimes the equivalent of 54 km per hour.

tiger's milk

2 shots cognac
pinch cinnamon
drop vanilla essence
¼ shot sugar syrup
1 shot double cream
1 shot milk
½ fresh egg white

Add all ingredients to a shaker. Shake with ice and strain into a glass filled with ice.

tom and jerry

2 shots golden rum
2 shots cognac
1 fresh egg white
1 fresh egg yolk
¼ shot sugar syrup
pinch cinnamon
top up with boiling water

Beat the egg white until stiff. In a separate bowl beat the yolk until runny. Mix them together and pour iinto a toddy glass. Add the rum, cognac, sugar and spices and stir the mixture. top up with boiling water.

tuscan mule

2 shots tuaca liqueur
1 shot freshly squeezed lime juice
top up with ginger beer

Shake the tuaca and lime juice with ice. Strain into a glass filled with ice and top up with the ginger beer.

utterly butterfly

2 shots vodka
½ shot malibu
2 shots apple juice
2 shots pineapple juice
½ shot freshly squeezed lime juice
1 spoon smooth peanut butter

Stir the peanut butter with the vodka in the base of a shaker. Add the other ingredients and shake with ice. Strain into a glass filled with ice.

(Right) Monarch butterflies are noted for their long annual migration. Beginning in August until the first frost they start off their massive southward journey in north America. From the following spring onwards a northward migration sees a return to their distant starting point. The monarch is the only butterfly that migrates both north and south in this way, but no single butterfly makes the entire round trip.

venus in fur

1 shot raspberry vodka
1 shot lemon vodka
3 shots apple juice
2 dashes angostura bitters

Add all ingredients to a shaker. Shake with ice and strain into a glass filled with ice.

(Right) During the summer months snow leopards live on mountainous meadows and rocky regions at altitudes above 2,700 feet. In the winter they come down into the forest areas at around 1,200 to 2000 feet. In this cold harsh habitat their thick fur, small round ears and stocky body all help to minimise heat loss as are their thickly covered tails, used as a blanket to protect the face when asleep.

Snow leopards are largely solitary animals, though mothers rear their young cubs for extended periods in mountain dens and like all big cats, feed by hunting. Snow leopards are not averse to taking livestock and to prevent them taking their animals herders will kill snow leopards. However snow leopards are known to be among the least aggressive of all big cats. They are easily driven away from livestock, abandon kills when threatened and sometimes do not even defend themselves when attacked.

white elephant

2 shots vodka
1 shot crème de cacao liqueur
1 shot double cream
1 shot milk

Add all ingredients to a shaker. Shake with ice and strain into a chilled martini glass. Dust with cocoa powder.

red rum martini

2 shots rum
½ shot sloe gin
½ shot freshly squeezed lemon juice
12 redcurrants
½ shot sugar syrup

Muddle the fruit in the base of the shaker. Add the remaining ingredients and shake with ice. Strain into a chilled martini glass. This cocktail is named after the great racing horse who went on to win the Grand National three times.

(Right) The most extraordinary feature of the elephant is its trunk, its 'super-nose'. With over sixty thousand muscles it is highly versatile, used for feeding, picking up grasses, leaves, fruits and leaves, and for drinking, where it can suck up between 135 and 225 litres of water a day. The trunk is also vital when it comes to bathing when an elephant will squirt water over its back to stay cool in high temperatures.

virgin bite of the iguana

1 shot freshly squeezed lime juice
1 shot freshly squeezed lemon juice
1 shot freshly squeezed orange juice
1 shot freshly squeezed tomato juice
1 handful cherry tomatoes, washed and halved
1 small clove garlic
1 teaspoon horseradish
2 to 3 dashes worcestershire sauce
lime wedge

Rub the rim of a chilled glass with the lime wedge and rim with salt. Add the remaining ingredients to a blender with ice. Blend until smooth and poor into a chilled glass. Squeeze the lime wedge over the drink and drop it in.

white lion

2 shots white rum
¼ shot cointreau
½ shot freshly squeezed lime juice
dash grenadine

Add all ingredients to a shaker. Shake with ice and strain into a chilled martini glass.

white spider

1 shot vodka
½ shot peppermint schnapps
(or white crème de menthe)
sprig fresh mint

Shake the vodka and schapps with ice. Strain into a chilled martini glass and garnish with the mint sprig. A perfect nightcap.

yellow bird

2 shots pineapple juice
1½ shots golden rum
½ shot crème de bananes liqueur
½ shot freshly squeezed lime juice
½ shot sugar syrup
¼ shot galliano

Add all ingredients to a shaker. Shake with ice and strain into a chilled martini glass.

the wolf

1 shot vodka
1 shot white crème de menthe liqueur
top up with lemonade

Pour the vodka and crème de menthe into an ice-filled highball glass. top up with the lemonade.

yellow parrot

1 shot apricot brandy
1 shot yellow chartreause
2 shots chilled mineral water
dash absinthe

Add all ingredients to a shaker. Shake with ice and strain into a chilled martini glass.

(Right) The wolf is largest member of the canine family. Gray wolves range in colour from a grizzled grey, to black or all white. All wolves are extremely sociable, traveling and hunting in a group or pack. This is usually a family a group, at its core a pairing of male and female and their offspring. Studies of wolf behaviour reveal their relationships and modes of communication to be complex and sophisticated.

zebra

1 shot white crème de cacao
2 shots kalhua

Carefully pour one shot of the kalhua into a chilled shot glass. Layer on top the crème de cacao and then finish with another layer of the kalhua. If desired, float a little cream on the surface.

(Left) It remains a mystery as to the reason why zebras should have such vividly striped coats. Animal behaviourists all disagree on the subject. Some believe the markings dazzle the lions, putting them off as they stake their prey. Others say that the stripes make it harder to distinguish one animal from another in the herd or that the stripes allow the zebras to discern their own herd from others. Another argument says the stripes prevent insects from landing and biting the zebra. Whatever the truth of it, the experts all agree that in behavioural terms the zebra is very much like a horse and like horses, they usually give birth to single foals. When it comes to mothers and their young, the bond that develops has to occur quickly in the wild where predators are always lurking. A foal is almost immediately on its feet and half an hour later it will trot readily along with the herd, getting to know the smell of its mother as she repeatedly licks him. As the days pass the zebra foal will recognize not only its mother, but each member of its herd, since every zebra has its own special pattern and no two are the same.

index